D1716109

THE LIVES OF GREAT ARTISTS

THE LIFE AND ART OF

CLAUDE MONET

THE LIVES OF GREAT ARTISTS
THE LIFE AND ART OF
CLAUDE MONET

SARA PAPPWORTH

ROSEN
PUBLISHING®
New York

This edition published in 2017 by

The Rosen Publishing Group, Inc.

29 East 21st Street

New York, NY 10010

Additional end matter copyright © 2017 by The Rosen Publishing Group, Inc.

Library of Congress Cataloging-in-Publication Data

Names: Pappworth, Sara, author. | Ryn, Aude van, illustrator.

Title: The life and art of Claude Monet / Sara Pappworth; illustrations by Aude Van Ryn.

Description: New York : Rosen Publishing, 2016. | Series: The lives of great artists | Includes bibliographical references and index.

Identifiers: LCCN 2016039107 | ISBN 9781499465846 (library bound)

Subjects: LCSH: Monet, Claude, 1840-1926—Juvenile literature. | Artists—France—Biography—Juvenile literature.

Classification: LCC N6853.M534 P37 2016 | DDC 759.4—dc23

LC record available at https://lccn.loc.gov/2016039107

Manufactured in the United States of America

© Text 2015 Annabel Howard. Annabel Howard has asserted her right, under the Copyright, Designs, and Patent Act 1988, to be identified as the Author of this Work.

© Illustrations 2015 Adam Simpson

Series editor: Catherine Ingram

This book was produced and published in 2015 by Laurence King Publishing Ltd., London.

Acknowledgements

To my mother, Jean Pappworth, who first inspired me to love Monet's paintings, and my children Joe, Tom and Katie who encouraged and advised me.

About the Author

Sara Pappworth is an art historian, teacher and photographer. She has taught in museums and galleries for more than twenty years and currently works at Tate Britain, Tate Modern, the Victoria & Albert Museum, the Wallace Collection and the National Gallery.

About the Illustrator

Aude Van Ryn studied at Central St Martins and the Royal College of Art in London. Her work has featured in theatre posters, packaging for Le Pain Quotidien and advertising campaigns for clients such as The British Heart Foundation. Her illustrations have featured in several exhibitions as well as shows for galleries in London and Tokyo.

Picture credits

All illustrations by Aude Van Ryn

8 Musée Marmottan Monet, Paris/Bridgeman Images 9 © The National Gallery, London/Scala, Florence 13 Kimbell Art Museum, Fort Worth, Texas/ Art Resource, NY/Scala, Florence 17 © Photo Josse, Paris 18 Allen Memorial Art Museum, Oberlin College, Ohio. R.T. Miller, Jr. Fund/Bridgeman Images 25 © The National Gallery, London/Scala, Florence 29 © Photo Josse, Paris 30, 34, 35 Musée Marmottan Monet, Paris/Bridgeman Images 37 White Images/Scala, Florence 38 Photo © Musée d'Orsay, Dist. RMN-Grand Palais/Patrice Schmidt 41 White Images/Scala, Florence 44 Image © The Metropolitan Museum of Art/Art Resource/Scala, Florence 49 DeAgostini Picture Library/Scala, Florence 52 Musée Marmottan Monet, Paris/ Bridgeman Images 55 Christie's Images, London/Scala, Florence 56 Photo The Philadelphia Museum of Art/Art Resource/Scala, Florence 59 © Paul M.R. Maeyaert 63 Musée Marmottan Monet, Paris/Bridgeman Images 64 © The National Gallery, London/Scala, Florence 65 Roger-Viollet/Topfoto 69 Private Collection/Bridgeman Images 73 © ARTOTHEK 71 Musée Marmottan Monet, Paris/Bridgeman Images 73 Minneapolis Institute of Arts, MN. Bequest of Putnam Dana McMillan/Bridgeman Images 78–79 Photo © RMN-Grand Palais (Musée de l'Orangerie)/Michel Urtado 81 Private Collection/Roger-Viollet, Paris/Bridgeman Images

Contents

Claude Monet, c. 1864
Photograph by Etienne Carjat

Oscar-Claude Monet is aged 22 in this photograph. He exudes great confidence; a self-assured young man who, though small, has a commanding presence. His cravat forms a deliberately bohemian, swaggering bow and we can detect a penetrating but kindly gaze. The youthful pout to his lower lip will soon be covered by the full beard that, in later years, dominates his face.

Monet is best known as a leading member of the French Impressionists, sharing their self-consciously modern subjects and style. This is a style to which he remained committed throughout his life. But his approach was unique and personal. He was never a follower and actively resisted rules and theories.

During the 86 years of his life Monet never rested. He was always driven by the urge to paint. More than 2,000 paintings remain from over six highly creative decades. The young Monet may have struggled for recognition and faced major financial difficulties, but by the time he reached middle age he was among the most successful artists ever known: a celebrity of his day. Despite his success, Monet never became complacent. He continued to paint into his seventies and eighties, evolving his art in new and astonishing ways.

Young Joker: Early Days 1840–58

Oscar-Claude Monet was born in Paris on November 14, 1840, a second son for Claude Adolphe, merchant seaman, and his musical wife, Louise-Justine. When Monet was 5 the family moved to Le Havre, where Monet's father joined his brother-in-law's successful wholesale grocery business. Monet loved living close to the sea and exploring the nearby countryside, but he found it hard to concentrate at school: "I covered my exercise books with highly irreverent drawings of my masters, full face or profile, with maximum distortion." By the age of 16 Monet had become so renowned for his caricatures that he later claimed to have earned significant sums drawing the people of Le Havre. Every Sunday five or so new caricatures were hung in a framer's shop window where the Le Havre townsfolk would gather and laugh when they recognized themselves or their friends.

Claude Monet

Petit Pantheon Theatral,
1860

Pencil on paper.
34 x 48 cm (13⅜ x 18⅞ in).
Musée Marmottan Monet, Paris.

Boudin's Inspirational Seascapes

Above Monet's caricatures the shop owner hung the small seascape paintings of a successful local artist, Eugène Boudin. Many years later Monet wrote, "I consider Boudin my master," but when, at the age of 15, Monet first met him, he dismissed the older artist and his seascapes with youthful arrogance. Then one day Boudin told him that he was wasting his talent making caricatures and challenged him to try and paint the local sea views instead. Monet later recalled this painting trip with Boudin: "I watched more attentively, and then it was as if a veil had been torn aside. ... I grasped what painting could be. ... You [Boudin] were the first to teach me to see and understand!"

Boudin's emphasis on painting outdoors, capturing light and weather effects, particularly by the sea, was to have a lasting influence on Monet. Indeed, Boudin had more direct influence on Monet's work than any subsequent teachers. By the time he exhibited, at the age of almost 18, alongside Boudin, in the annual Le Havre show, Monet was already committed to a subject and approach to painting that would come to dominate his later life.

Eugène Boudin

Beach Scene, Trouville,
c. 1870–74

Oil on wood.
18.2 x 46.2 cm (7⅛ x 18⅛ in).
National Gallery, London.

Out and About: Paris 1859–61

Boudin encouraged Monet to study at a Parisian atelier. These were the studios of successful artists who undertook to teach young apprentices. But despite Monet's early promise his father was not keen for him to pursue a career in painting. However, following the death of his mother, Monet's aunt (who had no children and some money) decided to support his choice of vocation. She agreed to help pay for his studies in Paris.

Monet may have been only 18 when he first arrived in Paris, but he was already displaying his characteristic determination to follow his own path. Instead of enrolling at one of the traditional ateliers, as Aunt Lecadre wanted, he opted to attend the more liberal Académie Suisse, where there was no formal instruction. Nevertheless, life models were available, the atmosphere was industrious and, above all, there was the inspiration to be found in the work of Monet's classmates, including Camille Pissaro, who was to become a fellow Impressionist and lifetime friend.

The few drawings and paintings that we have from this early stage of Monet's career demonstrate an extraordinarily precocious level of skill. Furthermore, judging from the letters that he sent Boudin, Monet clearly already had both a sophisticated understanding of what other artists were doing, and an interest in the art market. But perhaps Monet was a little over-confident, for it appears that much of his time was spent on another of his enduring interests: drinking and eating. Parisian café society was irresistible! His favourite haunt was the infamous Brasserie des Martyrs.

The Army

Monet's family were not impressed with his Parisian lifestyle. When he had the misfortune, in April 1861, to be conscripted into the army (something that the government conducted on a lottery basis) his family probably hoped that military discipline might teach him to mend his self-indulgent ways. But Monet appears to have seen the whole thing as an exciting artistic adventure. He opted to join the Chasseurs d'Afrique (First Regiment of African Light Cavalry). He wore a fabulous scarlet uniform, learned to ride a horse, and was posted to Algiers. Here he saw little, if any, action but, as he recalled many years later, "my vision gained so much … the impressions of light and colour that I received … [sowed] the seeds of my future experiments."

Monet's predicted seven years' army service was cut short after just over a year, when he caught typhoid fever and was sent home to convalesce in August 1862. Aunt Lecadre took pity on him and purchased his release from the regiment. As was the practice, she had to pay the substantial sum of 3,000 francs to buy a substitute soldier to take his place. She insisted that, in return, this time Monet should work hard and follow more conventional instruction in painting.

Back to Study and First Salon Success, 1862–65

Monet enrolled at the academy of Charles Gleyre, who was known for his preference for drawing over painting and the ideal over the real. He is said to have criticized Monet's life drawing on one occasion, saying, "You have given him the feet of a messenger boy!" When Monet retorted that he was just drawing what he saw, Gleyre replied that he should nevertheless always follow ideals of Classical beauty: "We must always have antiquity in mind." Despite this, Gleyre's academy was less strict than many, and consequently attracted some broad-minded students who were to prove the most important influence on Monet at this time. In particular, Frédéric Bazille, Pierre-Auguste Renoir, and Alfred Sisley were to become lifelong friends, and their association would ultimately lead to the foundation of Impressionism, some ten years later.

Meanwhile, Monet had to do something to convince Aunt Lecadre that her money was being well spent, and in Paris of the 1860s the only way to do that was to have your work accepted at the Paris Salon. Much as Monet and his friends abhorred the anti-progressive stance of the Salon jury – made up of an "in crowd" who only accepted highly conventional, idealized paintings – they had no choice but to apply. Worse still, the Salon favoured historical scenes and figurative subjects over landscapes and still lifes, which were considered far inferior. However, this was starting to change. In the 1830s a number of artists, such as Jean-Baptiste-Camille Corot and Théodore Rousseau, had begun to gain recognition specifically for their landscapes, and the young Monet decided to follow their lead by adopting the subject with which he felt most confident.

Monet submitted two seascapes to the 1865 Salon, one of which was *The Pointe de la Hève at Low Tide.* Here we can see that the 24-year-old already had exceptional talent. He describes the changeable weather of the Normandy coast with great skill – turquoise and azure light flashing on a brightly lit sea, above which hover dark descending clouds. Fortunately for Monet, both seascapes were accepted by the Salon and even received some critical praise.

The Pointe de la Hève at Low Tide

Claude Monet, 1865

Oil on canvas
90.2 x 150.5 cm (35½ x 59¼ in)
Kimbell Art Museum, Fort Worth, Texas

Poor Camille!

In 1866 Monet had more success at the Salon, with a landscape. Next he decided to raise the stakes and change to figure painting. The figure that he chose to paint again and again was that of 19-year-old model Camille-Léonie Doncieux. Camille's thick, long black hair and large dark eyes had inspired several young artists. For some reason (whether it was her temperament or situation is not clear), she was always referred to as "Poor Camille!"

By about 1866, Monet and Camille had started a relationship. Monet's 1866 painting of Camille shows her dressed in the latest fashion, standing against a plain, dark interior. This conventional portrait brought Monet more success at the Salon.

Following this, Monet planned a multi-figure subject in a garden, using Camille as the model for three of the four women in the composition. The canvas was massive as the figures were intended to be life-sized.

Monet decided that the painting needed to be made outdoors to show the real effects of exterior lighting, where the bright tones of the sun appear interspersed with blue tones cast by shady foliage. This presented practical difficulties, particularly with a canvas that was so large. So, rather than use a ladder, he dug a deep trench in the garden and attached the canvas to a pulley system that allowed him to hoist it up and down in order to reach all parts with relative ease.

Challenging Himself and Others

When Monet finally finished the work, he called it simply *Women in a Garden*. Although the figures' poses look rather contrived, the natural lighting on them is observed to a degree that had rarely, if ever, been seen before. Those who saw the painting expressed surprise at the blue colour of the shadows on the ladies' dresses. Weren't shadows always grey? "No!" was Monet's response; "look carefully and you will see that, in sunlight they can appear blue." The painting's title may sound innocuous, but at the time it represented a challenge to the Salon jury, who believed figurative art should show worthy historical narratives featuring famous people, not ordinary women, and that it should be contrived in the studio, not painted outdoors. Monet was also declaring allegiance to Édouard Manet and Gustave Courbet, older artists who had already caused a stir with paintings on similar themes, such as *Luncheon on the Grass* (Manet) and *Young Ladies on the Banks of the Seine* (Courbet). Throughout his life Monet was to set himself the challenge of going one step further on a theme already made important by predecessors.

Not surprisingly, the 1867 Salon rejected *Women in a Garden*. Monet's friends Renoir, Pissarro, Bazille, Sisley, and Paul Cézanne all had their work refused too, but their talk of organizing an alternative exhibition came to nothing. However, Bazille, who was quite wealthy, kindly agreed to buy *Women in a Garden* from Monet who, by this time, was beginning to experience financial difficulties.

Camille Monet, 1871
Photograph by Albert Greiner.

Claude Monet

The Garden of the Princess, Louvre

Claude Monet, 1867

Oil on canvas
91.8 x 61.9 cm (36⅛ x 24⅜ in)
Allen Memorial Art Museum, Oberlin College,
Ohio, USA/R.T. Miller, Jr. Fund

Painting Modern Life

Among Monet's circle of friends was Émile Zola, an influential critic as well as a progressive and successful realist novelist. Zola wrote admiringly of Monet's work and described him as "a man amid a crowd of eunuchs!" Zola also encouraged Monet and his friends to focus more on paintings of modern life.

From the mid-1800s Paris had been subject to a massive rebuilding program, designed to transform its cramped old streets with wide boulevards and open spaces. Inspired by the new urban landscape, Monet and Renoir worked together on a number of aerial views of the city. *The Garden of the Princess, Louvre* is one such painting. Here, this new urban environment is viewed as if seen through the lens of a camera, which was a new invention at that time. Instead of traditional perspective tricks, Monet now utilized contemporary photos, which showed this scene (and others like it) from viewpoints not previously seen in paintings. Strange angles appear, and cut-off edges are observed. People are like beetles, small, blurred black marks scurrying along at high speed: tiny anonymous creatures in this large, new metropolitan jungle. It is hard now to understand quite how daring and different such paintings would have seemed to Monet's contemporaries; Boudin wrote that he was amazed by "the audacity of his compositions." In both subject and style these paintings offered a fresh response to a new age.

Unfortunately, though, however hard Monet worked on producing numerous paintings in varied styles, he failed to make sufficient sales. Desperate letters remain from this time in which he exhorts his already patient friends to lend him more money. The problem, it transpired, was not simply one of accumulated debts. The need for money was made far more urgent by the prospect of two extra mouths to feed – Camille was pregnant. When Monet told his father and aunt, they were adamant that if he wanted their money he should have nothing to do with Camille (despite the fact that Claude Adolphe himself secretly had an illegitimate child). Monet was forced to live a double life. He stayed with his family in Le Havre, pretending to comply, while making frequent trips to see Camille in Paris.

Poor Monet!

These were hard times. All the demands of an unplanned family left Monet dealing with debtors. He bombarded his friends with letters detailing and complaining about his dire circumstances – and his wealthy friend Frédéric Bazille, in particular, would often cough up funds for the beleaguered young family.

"Poor Camille," pregnant, is left to cope on her own in Paris. Monet pays a medical student with a painting (a portrait of the student) to look after her while he is in Le Havre.

Other friends who received begging letters from Monet.

Auguste Renoir

Alfred Sisley

Paul Cézanne

Eugène Boudin

Frédéric Bazille

Émile Zola

Monet moves Camille and baby to the countryside. But they are soon thrown out of their new lodgings — he claimed, stark naked — for unpaid rent!

Baby Jean is born on August 8, 1867. Monet is surprised by his great feelings of affection for the child.

Monet considers throwing himself into the Seine in despair, but then thinks better of it.

The butcher and wine merchant and other debtors send officers to confiscate Monet's paintings — including some from exhibitions.

En Plein Air

Monet eventually moved with his new family to the countryside just outside Paris, where they could live more cheaply. Despite all his difficulties, Monet was constantly painting. He had no choice; inspired by the landscape he felt a compelling need to paint, and the more he painted, the more he was likely to earn enough money to get himself out of debt.

Monet painted outdoors, *en plein air* ("in the open air"), which was extremely unusual at this time. Famously, when asked, "But where is your studio?" Monet held up his hand and pointed to the fields around him, replying, "This is my studio!" Indeed, he saw it as a point of honour that he should paint "directly from nature." In this way he hoped to bring a greater naturalism and immediacy to his work – to allow whoever saw the paintings to feel as if they too were standing there, viewing the scene.

But there were a couple of major practical obstacles. First, in order to paint the landscape as it appeared directly in front of him, Monet had to record light and weather effects. But these were constantly changing. He was obliged to paint fast, using far bigger, bolder strokes than those of his predecessors, whose dainty, detailed descriptions were created in the studio. Even then, however fast Monet painted, he could never capture everything before the light or weather changed. He was therefore obliged to return, in the hope of capturing the exact same conditions. This was not always achievable so, contrary to his claim that he always painted *en plein air*, he sometimes had to finish an image in his studio. The other obstacle was the difficulty of painting outdoors, often in bad weather. The easel and canvases had to be carried, and Monet also had to attempt to protect himself from the elements, sometimes in winter using up to three coats, gloves, and a hot-water bottle for his feet. Even then, contemporary accounts claim they witnessed him painting with icicles growing off his beard, such was his dedication to painting outdoors.

Radical Tubes

However, there was one important invention that made painting *en plein air* far easier than it would have been earlier. In 1841 (the year after Monet was born) the invention of ready-made oil paint in metal tubes revolutionized painting. Previously artists had had to grind their own colours (made mostly from stones and minerals) and mix the dry powder with oil. The resulting oil paint was hard to transport (in pigs' bladders or glass containers) and the consistency meant that it was best applied thinly. But the Impressionists realized that the greater portability of the new pre-prepared paint would enable them to work outdoors. What's more, the paint could be squeezed onto the palette and applied quickly using thick, expressive brushstrokes thanks to another new invention, square-ended brushes. This new paint also came in a new range of bright colours. When these were combined with the light ground (underlayer) that Monet and his contemporaries used, their paintings acquired an iridescent quality that was completely unlike anything achieved by earlier artists, painting with duller colours on dark grounds.

"Without tubes of paint, there would have been no Impressionism."

Pierre-Auguste Renoir

Bathers at La Grenouillère, 1869

Monet's friend Renoir shared his interest in painting outdoors. Together they visited La Grenouillère, a newly popular leisure spot 7.5 miles (12 km) outside Paris made easily accessible by a new railway linking the city to the surrounding countryside. This gave Monet and Renoir the opportunity to paint *en plein air* and to paint modern life at one and the same place.

Monet painted a number of images of La Grenouillère, exploring different activities and viewpoints. He was clearly inspired by the subject (and perhaps by painting alongside Renoir), creating some of his most confident and original paintings to date. *Bathers at La Grenouillère* describes a place of recreation and pleasure, as people immerse themselves in the water, go boating, walking, or make their way to the waterside café which lies further along the jetty, just outside the painting. The trees reduce the sunlight's penetration, allowing for an effect of smoky shade and dappled light, interrupted by an occasional burst of colour: a lady in pink and red, a verdant green bush, and dabs of blue and white indicating reflected sky on the water. It is in the water that we see most clearly Monet's extraordinarily original, varied, and evocative brushstrokes, which vigorously and accurately describe not just what the water looks like, but also its very wateriness. A blob is used to show the distant swimmers, while longer, more structured strokes give shape and form to the boats. Each thing has its characteristic stroke and yet nothing is drawn – line and colour have become one. Monet submitted some of his Grenouillère paintings to the Salon in 1870. Once again they were rejected.

Franco–Prussian War

In June 1870 Camille Doncieux and Claude Monet finally married. It was a small affair, unattended by any close family. The marriage, taking place three years after Jean's birth, was perhaps to help Monet avoid military service in the hostilities developing between France and Prussia; married men were not the first to be conscripted. On July 19, 1870 France declared war on Prussia and its German allies. Contrary to French expectations, the Prussian forces were far superior. The war was over in less than a year and ended in a decisive defeat. As many as 150,000 French soldiers were killed or wounded, and Paris was besieged by the invading army, falling in January 1871. Then, soon after peace was declared and the Prussian army departed, there was a rebellion by a group of socialist-inspired Parisians known as the Paris Commune against the new French Republic. This rebellion was ruthlessly

put down, leading to the deaths of around 10,000 Parisians.

Bathers at La Grenouillère

Claude Monet, 1869

Oil on canvas
73 x 92 cm (28¼ x 36¼ in)
National Gallery, London. Bequeathed
by Mrs M.S. Walzer as part of the
Richard and Sophie Walzer Bequest

England

Paris's artistic community had mixed reactions to both of these catastrophic events. Bazille had enlisted in August 1870 and by November he was dead. Courbet was imprisoned for supporting the Paris Commune, helping to pull down the Vendôme Column, symbol of earlier imperial Napoleonic victories. But Monet himself and many of his friends took a more pragmatic – although, some would say, cowardly – approach. At some point, soon after war had been declared, Monet and his family slipped onto a boat and sailed across the Channel to the safety of England.

Monet found lodgings for the family in London and immediately began to paint. Predictably his favourite subjects were the parks and the River Thames. He also established what was to become a lifelong love of things British, particularly tweed and tea.

Monet met up with Pissarro, who was also in London, and they went together to the National Gallery where they admired John Constable's landscapes and J.M.W. Turner's seascapes. It has often been suggested that these had a major influence on Monet and, subsequently, the Impressionists. However, it appears more likely that the English artists' work simply provided confirmation of the importance of landscape painting based on careful observation of nature, colour, and light. Monet and Pissarro both also applied for inclusion in London's prestigious annual Royal Academy summer exhibition. But as had happened with the Salon, they were rejected. They were, however, included in a different London exhibition at a commercial gallery, organized by another French refugee, the art dealer Paul Durand-Ruel. This was to be the beginning of a long and prosperous relationship.

Holland

Artist friends in England had persuaded Monet that instead of returning home directly after the war he should first visit Holland. This involved numerous long boat journeys and poor Camille was very seasick. They arrived in June 1871 and remained for three months, during which time Monet worked in a "white heat" of enthusiasm. Staying in the north at Zaandam he was in his element, painting waterways, boats, and, above all, windmills.

Joy in Argenteuil

In autumn 1871 Monet returned with his family to Paris, where they took up residence near the Gare Saint-Lazare and met up with old friends. It does not appear that fleeing to England was held against Monet, perhaps because so many others did the same, or so few had been in favour of the war. However, it may in part have been the postwar hardships associated with living in Paris that caused Monet to follow Manet's advice and move out of the city to Argenteuil in December 1871.

Argenteuil was a small town next to the Seine, in the countryside but conveniently only 7.75 miles (12.5 km) from Paris and connected to it by train from the Gare Saint-Lazare. It was a picturesque spot, with much of its life centring on the river, its boats and bridges. Monet bought himself a boat and had it kitted out with a protective cabin and stand for his easel. This allowed him, whatever the weather, to explore the environs of Argenteuil and paint them from the river. He was extremely prolific. The landscape was an inspiration and he was also able to enjoy, for the first time, a degree of settled family life. Many of his friends were also living in the area. Renoir and Manet both painted several pictures of Monet and his family at this time. These show scenes of domestic contentment, with Camille sitting, skirt spread decoratively on the green grass, while Jean plays near the chickens and Monet potters in the garden. Monet also painted pictures of Camille and Jean, in which the sun always appears to be shining and harmony reigns. The colours are particularly bright and bold, with vermilion red dominating complementary greens. This more settled time in Argenteuil created an opportunity for Monet to explore a variety of techniques, including different types of brushstroke, unconventional compositions, and daring colour. Doubtless he discussed these techniques with his friends living nearby. They were to form the basis of Impressionism.

Poppies near Argenteuil

Claude Monet, 1873

Oil on canvas
50 x 65 cm (19⅝ x 25⅝ in)
Musée d'Orsay, Paris

Impression: Sunrise

Claude Monet, 1872

Oil on canvas

48 x 63 cm (19 x 24¾ in)

Musée Marmottan Monet, Paris

First Impressionist Exhibition, 1874

For years Monet, Renoir, Sisley, Berthe Morisot, Edgar Degas, Pissarro, and others had raged against the stranglehold that the Salon exerted, with its monopoly on opportunities for artists to exhibit and sell their work. Finally, they agreed to form themselves into the Société Anonyme and hold their own exhibition. There were to be more than 30 exhibitors, and it was an idealistic, egalitarian group. All work was to be given equal priority, hung alphabetically and all proceeds shared equally. Furthermore, there was no insistence on a particular group style. On April 15, 1874 the exhibition opened at a central studio space, belonging to the photographer Nadar. This was the first time that artists had come together to exhibit their work as a commercial enterprise, independent of the Salon and its jury selection system. It marked a massively important new development in ways artists could exhibit and sell, despite the fact that it was only open for a month, was poorly attended, and had minimal sales.

Monet exhibited five oil paintings and seven pastels, which were designed to show the range of his work. These included an urban street, viewed from the exhibition venue, a poppy field, a complex figure piece called *The Luncheon*, and a swiftly painted seascape, which at the last minute he named *Impression: Sunrise*. This title was chosen to indicate Monet's favoured approach of working "directly from nature with the aim of conveying my impressions in front of the most fugitive effects." It is a view of sunrise over Le Havre and was very daring in its open-ended brushstrokes, use of unpainted areas of canvas to create highlights, the inclusion of modern smoking factories, and the fluorescent orange of the sun. One critic, Louis Leroy, in an attempt to insult the exhibitors whose work he despised, took Monet's title and called them the Impressionists. The name stuck, but the insult did not. However, some visitors found the colours in the Impressionist paintings too bright. They feared the "alarming flickering light" and were worried that they would catch an eye disease!

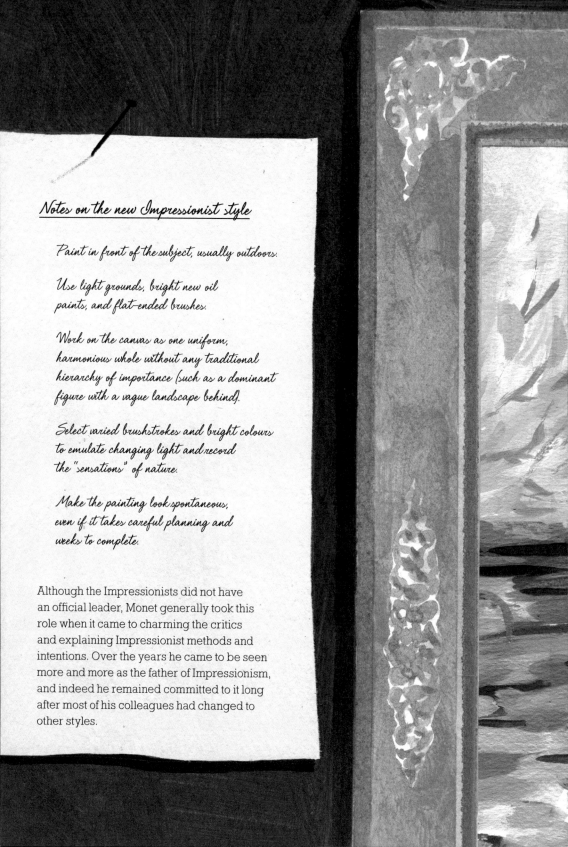

Notes on the new Impressionist style

Paint in front of the subject, usually outdoors.

Use light grounds, bright new oil paints, and flat-ended brushes.

Work on the canvas as one uniform, harmonious whole without any traditional hierarchy of importance (such as a dominant figure with a vague landscape behind).

Select varied brushstrokes and bright colours to emulate changing light and record the "sensations" of nature.

Make the painting look spontaneous, even if it takes careful planning and weeks to complete.

Although the Impressionists did not have an official leader, Monet generally took this role when it came to charming the critics and explaining Impressionist methods and intentions. Over the years he came to be seen more and more as the father of Impressionism, and indeed he remained committed to it long after most of his colleagues had changed to other styles.

Monet used his studio boat to explore the river and countryside around Argenteuil and find unusual viewpoints.

The Gare Saint-Lazare, 1877

Despite the limited success of their first exhibition, the Société Anonyme continued to exhibit together, and by their third show they had actually adopted the title of Impressionists. Now they were no longer an "Anonyme" collective but a named group. Ever the competitor, Monet made sure his work stood out by choosing to exhibit several paintings with an uncompromisingly modern subject, the Gare Saint-Lazare. This train station was at the epicentre of a newly modernized Paris and its links with the suburbs, beyond which Monet lived. Monet's paintings of it feature the recently invented steam trains, station buildings, signals, and crowds of commuters. Unusually, the challenges of capturing a constantly moving scene led Monet to make several preparatory drawings. He then painted 12 different views, using various sizes and shapes of canvas. In some, flashes of red and blue offset predominantly dark structures, while in others the steam submerges form to create a complex mosaic of diffused colour and light, like a "dreamworld." In keeping with his observation that pure black can rarely be seen, the apparent blacks of the trains and bridges in the Gare Saint-Lazare series are but a mixture of five different dark colours, rather than black.

Monet, ever the keen negotiator, persuaded the station staff to allow full access. They even agreed to delay a train to Rouen because "the light would be better then." This was indeed a man on a mission, a leader with gifted powers of persuasion!

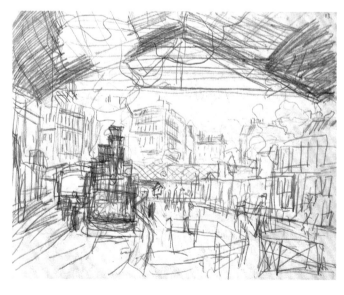

Claude Monet

Gare Saint-Lazare,
sketch of the interior, 1877

Pencil on paper.
25.5 x 34 cm (10 x 13⅜ in).
Musée Marmottan Monet, Paris.

Vive la France!

The date June 30, 1878 was declared a festival by France's government, as a symbol of recovery from the terrible defeat of the Franco–Prussian War. People were encouraged to decorate the streets with French flags, whose red, white, and blue dominate the colour scheme of Monet's painting *Rue Montorgueil*. His balcony viewpoint of this street in Paris leads to a dramatic composition in which bright colour and dynamic lines predominate, endowing this painting with a mood of energetic celebration. The style is stridently unconventional. Strong contrasting colours are used to model forms, and additional brightness is provided by a light background colour, which shines through. The crowd is conveyed through blurred shapes, like moving figures in a photograph. And the flags are painted using energetic flourishes, as if to indicate Monet's patriotic excitement at this new national celebration.

But critics continued to complain that such paintings appeared unfinished, and they struggled to see them from "the right viewpoint." "They are painted in such a way that if one goes up close to them one finds only scribbles of various colours." Nevertheless, the Impressionists continued to exhibit their work and, over time, critical reaction became more favourable. Although sales were still not as good as Monet hoped for, he did have some success with a few loyal buyers, notably the dealer Durand-Ruel, as well as a keen private collector, Ernest Hoschedé, who showed particular daring in purchasing *Impression: Sunrise* and three paintings of the Gare Saint-Lazare.

You can see it best from here!

Camille on her Deathbed
Claude Monet, 1879

Oil on canvas
90 x 68 cm (35½ x 26¾ in)

Families Can Be Complicated

Ernest Hoschedé was a Parisian merchant, art collector, and critic who had an extremely extravagant lifestyle. This was partly funded by his wealthy wife, Alice, whom he married when she was only 17. Six children swiftly followed. Alice inherited the grand Château de Rottembourg, near Paris, and here Ernest was able to indulge his passion for art, displaying the many paintings that he had bought, and commissioning new ones from both Manet and Monet, who was also asked to make some decorative panels for the chateau's dining room. Monet went to stay with the family and became intimate with them, particularly Alice. Meanwhile Ernest continued to be profligate, even paying for a private train to transport his guests from Paris to a party at the chateau. Eventually he was declared bankrupt. He owed more than two million francs to 151 creditors and the Hoschedé family was forced to leave their grand home. Monet was also having some financial difficulties, although they were far less pronounced. Furthermore, he was worried about Camille, who was very ill during her pregnancy with their second son, Michel, who was born in March 1878. It was decided that it would be to everyone's benefit if they took the unusual step of combining households. In the summer of 1878 the two families moved together into a rented house in Vétheuil, a rural area 42 miles (66 km) northwest of Paris.

Ernest was soon spending less time with his family, ostensibly pursuing new enterprises, which always failed. Letters between Alice and Ernest reveal that he was rarely in Vétheuil, not even making it for Christmas or the children's birthdays. Soon Monet found himself in charge of eight children and an extremely sick wife.

On September 5, 1879 Camille died. Monet wrote to a friend, "My poor wife gave up the struggle after the most ghastly suffering." Camille was only 32. Monet painted his beautiful wife one last time, on her deathbed; he couldn't help himself. As he observed, painting "is my day-long obsession, joy and torment to such an extent that ... I caught myself automatically searching ... the arrangement of coloured gradations that death was imposing on her motionless face. Blue, yellow, grey tones...."

Big Freeze, 1879–80

Soon after Camille's death the River Seine froze over as Paris and nearby Vétheuil experienced one of the coldest winters ever known. Despite his grief, Monet found inspiration in this dramatic landscape. He worked on 18 paintings at once, inspired by the frozen Seine and the thaw that followed, sending huge destructive blocks of ice (*glaçons*) crashing downriver.

At Christmas 1879, there was little money for food, let alone presents for Monet's newly enlarged family. But the terrible weather was making daily headlines and Monet must have been aware of the commercial potential of his choice of subject. So, when his paintings were rejected by the Salon, Monet decided to exhibit them himself. The exhibition took place at the premises of an avant-garde magazine, *La Vie Moderne*, in April 1880. It marked a new departure, a one-man exhibition on a single theme, with a catalogue that included an illustration by Manet and an important interview by Théodore Duret, who had recently published a book about the Impressionists. It was a commercial decision that paid off; several paintings sold, including *The Ice Floes*, which went for a record price. This exhibition represented a new beginning. From now on Monet would concentrate on painting landscapes and exhibiting in private galleries.

The painting style in *The Ice Floes* is more conventional, more finished looking, than earlier works, which probably contributed to its success. Furthermore, there is no sense of the havoc and destruction caused to humans and their property by the ice floes. Instead, Monet dwells on the landscape, its pastel colours, and the luminosity of early morning.

The Ice Floes

Claude Monet, 1880

Oil on canvas

Monet Likes *Monnaie*

After the success of his one-man show Monet was convinced that the way to exhibit his work was as part of an individually focused commercial venture, rather than the Salon or even the Impressionist exhibitions. There were a total of eight Impressionist exhibitions between 1874 and 1886. Increasingly, Monet did not take part. This was not uncommon, indeed Pissarro was the only artist to take part in every exhibition, but it did cause some resentment. Perhaps it was this, or jealousy at Monet's increasing commercial success, that caused Cézanne to observe, "Monet likes *monnaie*" (money)! And Degas scorned his "frantic self-advertising." But then again, they did not have eight children to feed. One colleague (who remained anonymous) felt so upset with Monet that he wrote a defamatory article in the journal *Le Gaulois*, in which he described Monet as dead to the art world and living in sin with Alice Hoschedé.

Over the next five years Monet did everything he could to increase his sales. Commercial galleries were a new phenomenon and it could be said that Monet was one of the first artists to appreciate their potential. The Durand-Ruel Gallery was the first to support Monet in the 1870s, but then it fell on hard times. In the early 1880s Paul Durand-Ruel renewed his interest in Monet, but would often operate by means of promissory notes or IOUs. Today's contractual obligation on an artist to commit to a gallery and vice versa did not exist. Monet appears to have had a keen commercial acumen. He realized that he could exploit this situation to his advantage. When Georges Petit invited him to exhibit at an "International Exhibition" he happily accepted. Likewise he was keen to welcome Vincent van Gogh's brother Theo to his home because Theo worked for the Goupil Gallery in Paris, for whom he bought several of Monet's paintings. As Monet became more successful, the galleries became increasingly anxious to sell his work, and he played them off against one another in order to increase his prices. But in the long term it was Durand-Ruel's constant commitment to Impressionism and his foresight in exhibiting Impressionist paintings in America (where a massive new market was opening up) that really convinced Monet, in later life, to sell the majority of his work through him.

"He Painted the Storm Amidst the Swirl of the Salt Water"

This is one critic's description of Monet painting along the Normandy coast. Between 1883 and 1886, Monet made more than 60 paintings inspired by this rugged coastline. They were hugely popular. He would go in the winter months when the weather was at its most dramatic and extreme. Courbet, Eugène Delacroix, and others had also painted this coastline, but typically Monet said, "I will try and do it differently."

Monet often recalled the following incident: "... absorbed as I was, I didn't see a big wave coming. It threw me against the cliff. I was tossed about in its wake along with all my materials. My immediate thought was that I was done for, as the water dragged me down, but in the end I managed to clamber out on all fours ... soaked through: the palette which I had kept a grip on had been knocked over my face and my beard was covered in yellow!"

In *The Manneporte* Monet adopts a dramatic and unusual view that could only be reached by squeezing down a long, dark tunnel. The form of the arch is reminiscent of rocks in Japanese prints such as those by Utagawa Kuniyoshi (1797–1861), whose work Monet admired and collected. The rock face is described by weaving thick slabs of colour together. The emphasis on emotional response and an expressive technique was very modern.

Confiding in Alice

A cynic might suggest that Monet's constant expeditions away from home were not only to seek inspiring subjects, but also to avoid the irksome chores associated with bringing up eight children. However, in one respect he was extremely dutiful. At the end of every day he sat down and wrote a letter to Alice. The main theme of these letters is not the children or his love for Alice, but the weather! Monet's days were completely dominated by his art, and his art was completely dominated by the weather. If it rained, or indeed if the sun shone too brightly, he would despair that this would prevent him from recording the same colours and atmosphere that he had started to paint on the previous day. Monet's letters are replete with such phrases as "utter despair," "I feel like throwing everything away," and "I'm so miserable," all because of the weather. But, in his own way Monet did appreciate having Alice to confide in – as he said, "it's consoling to talk about one's hardships." It is also interesting to note that although Alice (unlike Camille) is never seen in Monet's paintings, she does appear to have taken an active interest in his work, and her favourable response clearly mattered to him: "I feel when I am painting that I want to give you the pleasure of it. To let you see what I am seeing and that makes me do things well."

The long absences must have been hard for Alice and the children but the increased sales of the resulting paintings would have been a significant compensation. Although Monet was constantly on the move, the family were becoming increasingly settled, and when Monet came home he was able to enjoy greater domestic tranquillity. This is recorded in some of his paintings at this time, including *The Artist's Garden at Vétheuil*. This sun-filled scene shows the family's home, garden, and the youngest two children, Michel Monet and Jean-Pierre Hoschedé. Significantly, Monet refused to sell this large canvas, presumably because it reminded him of happy times with his family. Three years later, in 1883, the family moved to a more spacious house in Giverny. This was to become their final permanent home.

Bordighera

Claude Monet, 1884

Oil on canvas

65 x 80.8 cm (25⅝ x 31¹⁵⁄₁₆ in)

The Sun After the Storm

Alice was not the only one to whom Monet wrote letters complaining about the weather. His dealer, Paul Durand-Ruel, received similar letters, partly to offer excuses for late delivery of promised paintings. Frustrated, Durand-Ruel urged Monet to paint in the south of France, where the sunshine was more reliable. Monet agreed, and in December 1883 set off with Renoir for the Mediterranean coast. But Monet struggled to produce paintings that satisfied him. This should not have come as a surprise. He often took some time to feel that he had understood the best way to interpret a new place. There was also, he claimed, the additional problem that he "always worked better alone, from my own impressions." Thus when he returned to the Riviera, to Bordighera (on the Italian–French border), the following month he asked Durand-Ruel to keep his visit secret from Renoir. This second trip was a great success and by February 1884 he was writing to Alice, "Now I really feel the landscape: I can be bold and include every tone of pink and blue." Indeed, it is the vibrant colours and extravagant vegetation of the south that makes these paintings so striking and different. Monet retains his Impressionist style but the intense colours, which he claimed at first "appalled" him, and the variety of shapes within the lush vegetation, give a new boldness to his paintings.

New Kids on the Block

Monet made several trips to different parts of southern France, returning to Paris with paintings of "sweetness itself: white, pink, and blue all wrapped in this fairy-tale air." Not surprisingly these paintings sold well, including to Theo van Gogh, who bought ten of Antibes. For Monet this was also an opportunity to suggest the versatility of the Impressionist style at a time when it was becoming less popular among his fellow practitioners. The last Impressionist exhibition had been in 1886. Pissarro was following the example of a younger group of artists led by Georges Seurat and working in a Pointillist manner (the building up of an image by using small dots of pure colour). Likewise, Renoir had moved away from Impressionism, in his case towards a more traditional, classical style. Monet was becoming a minority with his continued use of Impressionist techniques. From being part of the avant-garde, he was now increasingly an establishment figure, and was even criticized as such by some younger artists.

A Retrospective, 1889

Monet's acceptance by the establishment came when he was invited to take part in a retrospective exhibition alongside France's premier sculptor, Auguste Rodin, who had recently received the Légion d'honneur for services to French art. Rodin was less excited by the prospect than Monet. He put his sculptures directly in front of Monet's paintings and said, "I don't give a damn about Monet … the only thing I care about is me!" When he came to Giverny to discuss the exhibition he looked so fierce that the frightened Hoschedé girls ran away.

The Monet and Hoschedé children enjoyed helping Monet. When Monet was working on several paintings at once, the children would carry them for him in a wheelbarrow. Monet would also ask them to model. Suzanne Hoschedé once fainted because she had to stand so long! Sometimes Monet taught her sister Blanche to paint.

Père Poly

Claude Monet, 1886

Oil on canvas
74 x 53 cm (29⅛ x 20⅞ in)
Musée Marmottan Monet, Paris

Seascapes, Portraits, and Still Lifes

During the 1880s Monet was constantly travelling. When he was not in southern France he was off visiting Holland's tulip fields, the dramatic volcanic landscapes of the Massif Central, or continuing to explore new aspects of his beloved Normandy and Brittany coasts. It was almost as if, every year, he needed another dose of sea air. He even said that he wanted to be buried in a buoy. "Only the sea made Monsieur Monet happy. He needed water, great quantities of it, and the more there was of it, even if it was spattering our faces with foam, the better pleased he was," recalled one local friend, Père Poly, a Brittany-based fisherman. He became Monet's porter, carrying his canvases for miles while Monet hiked up treacherous cliff paths to find the perfect view.

Poly also became the subject of one of Monet's infrequent portraits. Here we can still see the caricaturist's eye in the pronounced nose and wayward facial hair. The Impressionist-style energetic brushstrokes so often used to describe the sea work equally well here to indicate the bulk of his fisherman's sweater and the force of his quizzical gaze. Unusually, this painting is signed prominently in red: "Claude Monet, Belle Isle 86." Clearly this man and this place were important to him. Monet hung *Père Poly* at home, above his desk. When the weather was too bad to paint outdoors Monet would paint portraits or still lifes.

Don't get annoyed, paint these!

Series of Stacks

In 1888 Monet started to paint a new subject, which was closer to home. It was the grain stacks that dominated the fields near his house in Giverny. Yet again Monet had a famous predecessor in his choice of subject: Jean-François Millet, who included stacks of grain in his paintings as symbols of the benevolence of God and man's harmony with nature. Millet's paintings had become a source of national pride, and when one happened to be sold to an American collector, the French government bought it back, with the President himself greeting its return to France. Human presence and spiritual elation in Monet's so-called haystack paintings (they are, in fact, grain stacks) are implied rather than described. Monet focuses on capturing the visual effects of colour and light as they interact and change with different seasons and at different times of day. In a letter of 1890 he states: "I'm hard at it … but at this time of the year the sun sets so fast that I can't keep up … a lot of work has to be done in order to render what I'd call 'instantaneity' [and] I'm disgusted by easy things that come in one go."

For more than three years Monet painted grain stacks. Working on several canvases at once, moving from one to the next as the light changed, he captured what he thought of as the unifying "envelope" of light with layers of small, fragmented brushstrokes. Their harmonious colours and flickering sparks describe not only a moment but also his emotional response to it. These paintings may also have been a challenge, or response, to the different, quasi-scientific approach that the younger Pointillists adopted when they too explored the interactions of colour and light.

Claude Monet

Grain Stacks, Snow Effect, Morning, 1891

Oil on canvas.
64.8 x 99.7 cm (25½ x 39¼ in).
J. Paul Getty Museum, Los Angeles.

Grain Stacks,
Pink and Blue Impressions

Claude Monet, 1891

Oil on canvas
c. 73 x 92 cm (28¼ x 36¼ in)
Private Collection, London

Decorative Poplars

In 1890 Monet was able to buy the house he had been renting in Giverny. In May 1891 he exhibited his series of grain stacks to great critical acclaim and achieved substantial sales. From this time Monet felt encouraged to focus on painting series and working closer to home. So, after the stacks he took his studio boat along a small river bordering the Giverny property, and made 24 paintings of a curving line of poplar trees. From this viewpoint we look up at the dancing forms of the trees and their reflections in the water, as they curve back into the distance. These natural arabesque designs are reminiscent of the Art Nouveau style (which was just becoming popular in French decorative arts at this time), while the adventurous compositions, with flattened shapes and cut-offs, may also show the influence of Monet's beloved Japanese woodcuts.

Once again, Monet painted in different lights and seasons to create this series, but this time he encountered a man-made problem. Poplars are commonly grown in France as windbreaks and for their wood. When Monet was partway through the series he was appalled to learn that the trees he was painting were to be harvested. In the end he bought the trees at auction, later selling them to a timber merchant once his paintings were finished.

While he worked on the grain stacks and the poplars, Monet evolved a notion of working on his series of paintings as a single unit. After making the paintings *en plein air* he took them back to his studio at Giverny, lined them up, and adjusted them, finishing off each painting in relation to the next, to create one harmonious whole. No paintings were sold prior to exhibition and it was with some reluctance that Monet split them up for sale individually.

Rouen Cathedral

"Dear God, this cathedral is hard to do!" Monet moaned to Alice. He had chosen the subject when visiting his brother, who lived in Rouen. From 1892 to 1894 he struggled to paint the cathedral, searching for the best viewpoint, the ideal weather and seeking to capture the changing light as he worked on more than 30 images. To get his views, Monet painted from the windows of adjacent shops, including from a ladies' dressing room. He said of this series,
"I want to do architecture without using lines or contours." Indeed, the majestic building is modelled by warm pinks, which appear to come forward, cool blues that appear to recede, and layers of thick impasto paint, which give an extraordinary palpability to this evocation of solid stone. The whole is a contradictory mixture of vagueness and definition, of harmony and contrast. The effect is sublime; spiritual without being religious, an ode to the beauty of French Gothic architecture, without being overtly patriotic.

When the Rouen Cathedral series was exhibited at Durand-Ruel's gallery it was praised by critics and by fellow artists. Cézanne commented perceptively: "It is the work of a determined man, carefully thought out, trying for the most subtle and elusive effects." The paintings sold for more than five times the prices achieved for the grain stacks and poplars. What gave them such appeal? Was it the subject, with its elements of religion and patriotism, or was it that Monet was now well and truly established as the leading artist of his day?

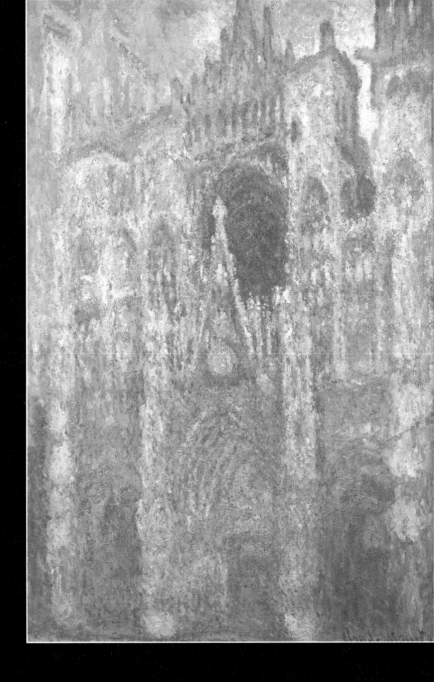

Rouen Cathedral,
Portal, Morning Sun,
Harmony in Blue
Claude Monet, 1893

Oil on canvas
92.2 x 63 cm (36⅛ x 24¼ in)
Musée d'Orsay, Paris

The Garden at Giverny

After buying the Giverny house in 1890 Monet spent more time there and set about improving the studio spaces and, above all, the garden. In 1893 he bought some additional land, which became the site for a lily pond, surmounted by a Japanese-style bridge. Monet married Alice in 1892, following the death of Ernest Hoschedé. Enjoying his increased wealth and domestic security, Monet immersed himself in the creation of a beautiful and tranquil domestic haven.

"It Is the Surrounding Atmosphere Which Gives Objects their Real Value"

Spending more time in Giverny also meant an opportunity for Monet to paint with far more ease. Local scenes were familiar and in close proximity to his studio. This made life physically easier for a man in his fifties, and had the additional practical advantages that he no longer had to waste time choosing motifs, or having his work disrupted for up to a year by changes in the weather. But Monet continued to push himself hard, getting up as early as 3:30 am to catch the summer sunrise over the River Seine. Between 1896 and 1897 this scene formed a series called Mornings on the Seine, in which each canvas records the progression of changing light and atmosphere as the sun rises. In these works, painted from his studio boat, Monet suggests the iridescent quality of dawn light on soft tree forms reflected in water. Monet must have been aware that the misty suggestiveness of these paintings is similar to those made by French landscape's founding fathers Claude Lorrain (c. 1600–82) and Camille Corot (1796–1875).

It is typical of Monet's later work that in *Branch of the Seine, near Giverny* he focuses on a single motif, free from any human presence. Instead, the emphasis is on nature, particularly its abstract and poetic qualities. The horizon line comes nearly halfway down the unusually square format of the canvas, creating an almost exact symmetry of "reality" and its reflection. You could turn the painting upside down and it would be much the same. Nothing disturbs the sense of contemplative calm. Even the paint texture is smoother and more uniform. Despite Monet's agnosticism it is possible to detect in such paintings a sense of what his Symbolist poet friend Stéphane Mallarmé called a search for the "mystery" of the divine or, as Pissarro described it, a feeling that "salvation lies in nature."

Branch of the Seine, near Giverny

Claude Monet, 1897

Oil on canvas
89 x 91 cm (35 x 35⅞ in)
Musée Marmottan Monet, Paris

The Water Lily Pond

Claude Monet, 1899

Oil on canvas

88.3 x 93.1 cm (34¾ x 36⅝ in)

Local Celebrity

In Giverny, Monet became something of a local celebrity when he purchased some land to stop the building of factories adjacent to the village. He also paid for school prizes and a playground. Such generous actions were not entirely without self-interest. Monet gained support from the mayor, who consequently rebuffed villagers' complaints regarding the diversion of a local river to feed Monet's lily pond.

Turn of the Century

"So much pain and heartache … and yet I must be strong and console my loved ones." Thus wrote Monet after the death in 1899 of Alice's daughter and his favourite model, Suzanne, at the age of 35, following a long illness. Alice was extremely depressed. Monet stayed by her side and sat in his burgeoning garden, painting. By this time the lilies had finally become established in the pond and wisteria was spreading across the Japanese bridge. It was irresistible. Between 1899 and 1900 Monet painted 18 views of the bridge, many of which adopt the same square format and symmetry as the Mornings on the Seine series. But now the space has become more compressed as thick, bright green paint marks the surface with horizontal bands of merging pads, bridge and foliage. We can imagine ourselves standing on the bridge, under the willow canopy, meditating on these tranquil and harmonious waters.

Monet with his friend, the statesman Georges Clémenceau, on the Japanese bridge at Giverny, 1921

Clémenceau – who led the French government during World War I – was a close friend from the 1890s onwards.

Foggy London

Over three winters from 1899 to 1901 Monet worked on nearly 100 views of London, many featuring the River Thames. Monet was a great Anglophile. He sent both his sons to study in England and enjoyed wearing tweed, drinking tea, and dining with English aristocrats. When in London he occupied a grand room at the Savoy Hotel, from where he could see the river.

His river views of the city are possibly a response to scenes made famous by two artists he admired – J.M.W. Turner and James McNeill Whistler. London's pollution was also an attraction. Coal smoke from domestic fires and industrial furnaces led to spectacular, colour-filled fogs.

However, painting in London proved difficult. He complained, "This is not a country where you can finish a painting on the spot – the effects never reappear!" In 1904 Monet exhibited 37 of his almost abstract London paintings. He commented, "No one would ever guess the trouble I'd gone through to end up with so little!," but they were a great success.

Bon Viveur

Monet's income was now 300 times that of a Parisian labourer. He had several house servants and seven gardeners. In 1900 he bought a new car and even hired a chauffeur to drive it. Driving became the family passion.

Everybody's Friend

As Monet's reputation increased he exhibited widely abroad, including in America, Italy, Germany, and Russia, and he had increasing numbers of visitors to Giverny. A small colony of American followers even settled nearby. But throughout his life and despite his success, Monet continued to support his less fortunate artist friends. He lent money to Pissarro, supported Sisley's family after he died, bought paintings from struggling friends such as Cézanne and Berthe Morisot, and campaigned for Manet and Gustave Caillebotte's paintings to be exhibited in national galleries. He also supported his friend Zola when he controversially defended Alfred Dreyfus, an army officer falsely accused by anti-Semites of treason in a case that caused nationwide turmoil. Furthermore, despite enjoying an affluent lifestyle, Monet appears to have been quite modest. He even turned down the Légion d'honneur.

The First Lilies

Monet's success and increasing years did not cause him to slow down. On the contrary, from the age of 60 in 1900 until his death in 1926, he made more paintings on average per year than before. In particular, he worked on images of his water lily pond, which he had extended in 1903, and which he thought of as "landscapes of water and reflection," admitting that they "became an obsession." This carefully orchestrated man-made landscape – pond, bridge, lilies, and surrounding vegetation – is a long way from the raw power of nature of his earlier seascapes. Instead, Monet focuses on controlled calm, while also experimenting with composition and format. (He also created some circular paintings.) Above all, these paintings feature an upside-down world: now everything is below the horizon and nearly everything is seen as its reflection in the water. The viewpoint to achieve this is unusual too. It seems that he would have had to lie on his stomach at the edge of the pond, looking above and across the water.

In 1909 Monet exhibited 48 water lily paintings. They were universally acclaimed. As one critic wrote: "One has never seen anything like it … beautiful to a degree which one can hardly express without seeming to exaggerate."

Santa Maria della Salute, Venice

Claude Monet, 1908

Oil on canvas
73.5 x 92.5 cm (29 x 36⅜ in)
Private Collection

"Venice Has Got Hold of Him and Won't Let Go!"

So exclaimed Alice when, on a rare occasion in 1908, she accompanied her husband on a painting trip. "My only worry is that he might tire himself. I have spent some unforgettable days here at the side of my husband, following every movement of his brush." It was impossible, it seems, for Monet to have a holiday without prioritizing work, but he did do some sightseeing with Alice and enjoyed the opportunity to paint from a gondola, which led to some surprising viewpoints with cropped objects and strange angles. Nevertheless, as usual he struggled when first exploring this new subject and complained that it was "too beautiful to be painted." In *Santa Maria della Salute, Venice*, the watery mists of a warmer climate fuse with glowing pinks and strident mauves. The romantic domes are viewed to one side, behind strong, vertical poles and gently lapping waves. As with the London series, Monet took the Venice paintings home to finish in his studio.

Sadly, in May 1911, after a painful illness, Alice died. They had been together for more than 30 years. Monet was heartbroken. For the only time in his life he struggled to paint. It was with great reluctance that he put the finishing touches to his Venice paintings, which inevitably reminded him of happier times together. These were exhibited in 1912. But for nearly two years afterwards he felt so depressed and full of self-doubt that he made barely half a dozen paintings. As he told Durand-Ruel: "age and sorrow have drained my strength ... more than ever today, I realize how artificial is this undeserved fame I have won."

*Monet and Alice in
St. Mark's Square,
Venice,* 1908
Musée Marmottan Monet, Paris.

Changing Perceptions

Monet's painting difficulties were compounded from 1912 by problems with his eyesight. He was diagnosed with double cataracts and sought solutions through various treatments, including eye drops and specially made glasses. These glasses used different-coloured lenses to compensate for Monet's tendency to see everything with a yellow tinge.

Whenever a treatment led to a temporary improvement in Monet's sight he felt a renewed sense of urgency: "I am working hard and I would like to paint everything before not being able to see anything any more." As well as painting his pond he also explored other areas of the garden, which had now matured to form colourful blooms throughout the year. In some of these paintings it is clear that Monet's eye problems affected his ability to see clearly, as well as his perception of colour. In his c. 1919–24 painting of the Japanese bridge covered in wisteria, for example, the colour has become strange and unnatural, with yellow dominating. Brushstrokes appear to be making a frenzied but unsuccessful effort to define forms that become increasingly unclear as more layers of thick paint are applied. Indeed, the paint is so thick in places that it looks almost as if it has been thrown onto the canvas, while in other areas Monet's brush carves deep ridges into the mountains of colour. Viewed from a distance the bridge can be discerned, but close up the thick encrustations of paint make it look more carved than painted. In 1923 a cataract operation on one eye helped Monet to see a little more clearly.

The Japanese Bridge

Claude Monet, c. 1919–24

Oil on canvas
89 x 116 cm (35 x 45¾ in)
Minneapolis Institute of Arts, Minnesota.
Bequest of Putnam Dana McMillan

Unsigned and Unsatisfactory

Monet's poor eyesight was one of the reasons that in his later years he took longer to complete his paintings, and quite often even failed to finish them. He had always been his own worst critic, prone to destroying his work if he was unhappy with it. Now, as his eyes deteriorated, he appears to have felt less secure about his judgement, so he also tended to frequently rework his paintings, sometimes over several years. In addition, he felt less urgency to complete paintings because he had no financial need to do so. Thus Monet's response to Durand-Ruel pressurizing him for more paintings was to tell him that he did not wish to turn into "a mere painting machine," and he "resolved never again to sell anything that I find just all right." Of one thing he was certain, he was not seeking "polish," but he did recognize that finding the perfect balance between a finished and a spontaneous appearance was not always easy and so, like many artists, he was not always certain that he had definitely reached the point when an individual work had been completed. When he was sure, he signed his work. However, many paintings from Monet's later years, which he never signed, exist in major art galleries.

Death, War, and New Beginnings

When, after Monet's initial Water Lilies exhibition in 1909, the series was broken up to be sold, friends and critics suggested that a permanent, public exhibition should be created to display any future water lilies, or *Nymphéas*. Several years later, at a time of great personal and national tragedy, the idea was revived. In February 1914 Monet's eldest son Jean died after a long illness. Then, in July 1914, World War I broke out. German troops were not far from Giverny. Strangely, the declaration of war appears to have given Monet the impetus to start his new Water Lilies series, after a period of virtual inactivity following the deaths of Alice and Jean. As he told Durand-Ruel, "I've started work again and you know I don't do things by halves: getting up at four in the morning, I slave away all day." This was his most ambitious series to date: to create some enormous water lily paintings for the proposed permanent, public display. In preparation Monet painted nearly 100 Water Lilies over 12 years, between 1914 and 1926. Most are horizontal format and many are up to 16 feet (5 meters) wide. Monet had a special studio built to house them. The paintings were attached to giant easels on wheels, so that he could work on several at the same time and adjust how one related to another.

The Orangerie

Created at a time of personal bereavement and the war, the Water Lilies could be seen as a kind of elegy for the dead, a muted, soft, colour-filled mourning, comparable to Gabriel Fauré's *Requiem* of some 20 years earlier. But the Water Lilies also seem full of hope and consolation, and Monet himself hoped that for those visiting the exhibition their "overworked and strained nerves could be released in keeping with the restful mood of the sleepy waters … the room could offer a refuge for peaceful meditation."

Georges Clémenceau, Monet's friend and a senior politician, promised in 1916 that the State would create a special building in Paris to house the Water Lilies. In return, Monet agreed to donate them. The initial plan of constructing an elliptically shaped building proved too expensive, and, after much debate, the Orangerie (formerly a grand conservatory with orange trees) in Paris's Tuileries Garden was adapted to create two oval rooms in which a selection of eight canvases could be displayed.

However, there was so much prevarication about which works to choose, and what order to show them in, that the Water Lilies exhibit at the Orangerie did not finally open until a few months after Monet's death. The installation of the eight enormous water lily paintings remains today. The huge canvases are hung just off the ground, hovering at eye level, surrounding the viewer with water and lilies.

Colour and Light

As so often before, Monet was ahead of his time. He had created an art installation in which the viewer becomes an active participant. The discreet arched openings between the two rooms add to the sense of flow.

The larger room contains views of the lily pond seen at different times of day. Colours range from the dusty blues and mauves of early morning to the blazing yellows and oranges of a sunset. The lily pads are what Monet called "just an accompaniment. The essence of the motif is the mirror of water, whose appearance alters at every moment." In the smaller room the perspective changes as we view the water at a greater distance, from behind the dark vertical trunks and fluttering branch curtains of weeping willow trees and their reflections. The colours are a more uniform mixture of blues, mauves, and deep, dark plum interspersed with green.

One of the most extraordinary aspects of the *Nymphéas* is the vigour with which they are painted, and the variety of brush marks. There is a sense of urgency in these enormous canvases, which are covered with often intense and unusual colours. These create the illusion of depth, as brighter colours appear to come forward while darker ones recede. Each colour harmonizes with the next as they are built up in layers of matt paint, one hue blending into another to create this colourful symphony.

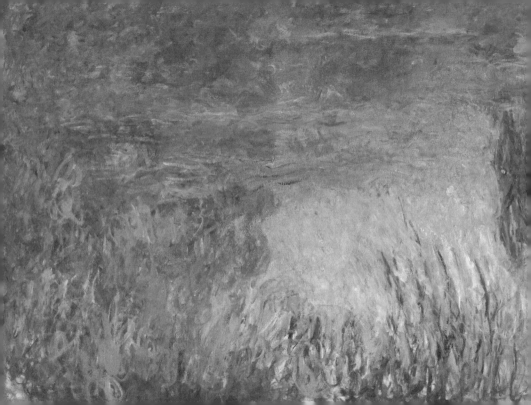

Clémenceau observed that Monet continued to work on his Water Lilies "as if he had all eternity before him." But on December 5, 1926 Monet died, aged 86. His death made news headlines, but with characteristic modesty he had asked for a quiet funeral, with no religious ceremony or speeches. Clémenceau, on seeing his friend's coffin draped in black, is said to have declared, "No black for Monet!" and replaced it with a floral cloth.

Monet had an instinctive aesthetic and emotional response to his subject. Despite his exploration of new painting techniques, his work never had its basis in artistic theories. As Monet said, "I do what I can to convey what I experience before nature and … most often in order to succeed in conveying what I feel, I totally forget the most elementary rules of painting, if they exist." Over the years his need to "fix sensations" and capture fugitive, changing effects, increasingly became the central obsession of his art. In the process, less became more, as he turned from complex images to focus on single motifs.

In the nineteenth century Monet was a leader of a highly influential, avant-garde group – the Impressionists. In the twentieth century his influence was felt again by a new generation of artists. Many of them (including the Abstract Expressionists) particularly admired Monet's later work for its use of abstraction, gestural strokes, expressive colour, and massive scale. Few artists can have had such an impact on so many, over so many years. But Monet's influence goes beyond his art. Who, having seen his paintings, does not feel their resonance? Will a water lily or a grain stack, for example, not be seen through Monet's eyes ever after? As Monet said to Clémenceau: "I have looked at what the universe has shown, to bear witness to it through my paintbrush. Put your hand in mine and let us help one another to see things better."

Glossary

ABSTRACT Expressing ideas and emotions by using elements such as colors and lines without attempting to create a realistic picture; having only intrinsic form with little or no attempt at pictorial representation or narrative content.

ABSTRACT EXPRESSIONISM An artistic movement of the mid-20th century comprising diverse styles and techniques and emphasizing especially an artist's liberty to convey attitudes and emotions through nontraditional and usually nonrepresentational means.

AESTHETIC Of, relating to, or dealing with art or the beautiful; artistic; pleasing in appearance; attractive; appreciative of, responsive to, or zealous about the beautiful; responsive to or appreciative of what is pleasurable to the senses.

AVANT-GARDE A group of people who develop new and often very surprising ideas in art, literature, etc.

COLLECTIVE Denoting a number of persons or things considered as one group or whole; involving all members of a group as distinct from its individuals; shared or assumed by all members of the group.

EASEL A frame for supporting an artist's painting.

EN PLEIN AIR In the open air; outdoors.

ESTABLISHMENT An established order of society; a group of social, economic, and political leaders who form a ruling class (as of a nation); a controlling group.

FIGURATIVE Showing people and things in a way that resembles how they really look; not abstract; of or relating to representation of form or figure in art.

IMPRESSIONISM A theory or practice in painting especially among French painters of about 1870 of depicting the natural appearances of objects by means of dabs or strokes of primary unmixed colors in order to simulate actual reflected light; the depiction (as in literature) of scene, emotion, or character by details intended to achieve a vividness or effectiveness more by evoking subjective and sensory impressions than by recreating an objective reality.

NATURALISM Realism in art or literature; a style of art or literature that shows people and things as they actually are.

PALETTE A thin oval or rectangular board or tablet that a painter holds and mixes pigments on; the set of colors put on the palette; a particular range, quality, or use of color.

RETROSPECTIVE An exhibition or compilation showing the development of the work of a particular artist over a period of time.

SALON A fashionable assemblage of notables (as literary figures, artists, or statesmen) held by custom at the home of a prominent person; a hall for exhibition of art; an annual exhibition of works of art.

SYMBOLIST One of a group of writers and artists in France after 1880 reacting against realism, concerning themselves with general truths instead of actualities, exalting the metaphysical and the mysterious, and aiming to unify and blend the arts and the functions of the senses.

For More Information

Art Institute of Chicago

111 South Michigan Avenue

Chicago, IL 60603-6404

Website: http://www.artic.edu

The Art Institute of Chicago collects, preserves, and interprets works of art of the highest quality, representing the world's diverse artistic traditions, for the inspiration and education of the public and in accordance with the profession's highest ethical standards and practices.

The Getty

1200 Getty Center Drive

Los Angeles, CA 90049-1679

(310) 440-7300

Website: http://www.getty.edu

The J. Paul Getty Trust is a cultural and philanthropic institution dedicated to the presentation, conservation, and interpretation of the world's artistic legacy. The Getty is dedicated to the proposition that works of art are windows onto the world's diverse and intertwined histories, mirrors of humanity's innate imagination and creativity, and inspiration to envision the future.

The Metropolitan Museum of Art

1000 Fifth Avenue

New York, NY 10028

(212) 535-7710

Website: http://www.metmuseum.org

The Metropolitan Museum of Art collects, studies, conserves, and presents significant works of art across all times and cultures in order to connect people to creativity, knowledge, and ideas. The Met presents over 5,000 years of art from around the world for everyone to experience and enjoy. The Museum lives in three iconic sites in New York City—The Met Fifth Avenue, The Met Breuer, and The Met Cloisters. Millions of people also take part in The Met experience online.

Musée Marmottan Monet

2 Rue Louis Boilly

Paris, France 75016

Website: http://www.marmottan.fr/uk

The Musée Marmottan Monet owns the largest Monet collection in the world. This collection, presented in a room specially built for this purpose, gives the public the unique opportunity to admire all the significant stages of the master painter's career and follow the evolution of his technique, from his youthful caricatures of Le Havre's personalities or Parisian critics to the paintings inspired by his Giverny garden.

The Museum of Modern Art (MoMA)

11 West 53rd Street

New York, NY 10019

(212) 708-9400

Website: https://www.moma.org

Founded in 1929 as an educational institution, The Museum of Modern Art is dedicated to being the foremost museum of modern art in the world. Through the leadership of its Trustees and staff, The Museum of Modern Art manifests this commitment by establishing, preserving, and documenting a permanent collection of the highest order that reflects the vitality, complexity, and unfolding patterns of modern and contemporary art and by presenting exhibitions and educational programs of unparalleled significance. Central to The Museum of Modern Art's mission is the encouragement of an ever-deeper understanding and enjoyment of modern and contemporary art by the diverse local, national, and international audiences that it serves.

WEBSITES

Because of the changing nature of internet links, Rosen Publishing has developed an online list of websites related to the subject of this book. This site is updated regularly. Please use this link to access this list:

http://www.rosenlinks.com/LGA/monet

For Further Reading

Fell, Derek. *The Magic of Monet's Garden: His Planting Plans and Color Harmonies.* New York, NY: Firefly Books, 2017.

Gilson, Jean-Pierre. *Claude Monet's Gardens at Giverny*. New York, NY: Harry N. Abrams, 2013.

Hodge, Susie. *Monet: His Life and Works in 500 Images.* London, England: Lorenz Books, 2010.

King, Ross. *Mad Enchantment: Claude Monet and the Painting of Water Lilies.* New York, NY: Bloomsbury USA, 2016.

Kramer, Felix, ed. *Monet and the Birth of Impressionism.* London, England: Prestel, 2015.

Murray, Elizabeth. *Monet's Passion: Ideas, Inspiration, and Insights from the Painter's Gardens.* Petaluma, CA: Pomegranate, 2010.

Russell, Vivian. *Monet's Garden: Through the Seasons at Giverny.* London, England: Frances Lincoln, 2016.

Wildenstein, Daniel. *Monet, or the Triumph of Impressionism.* Cologne, Germany: Taschen, 2014.

Bibliography

Brettell, Rchard R. *Impression: Painting Quickly in France, 1860–90*. New Haven, CT: Yale University Press, 2000.

Clarke, Michae,l and Richard Thomson. *Monet, The Seine and The Sea. Edinburgh, Scotland:* National Galleries of Scotland, 2006.

Dixon, Annette, Carole McNamara, and Charles Stuckey. *Monet at Vétheuil: The Turning Point. Ann Arbor, MI:* University of Michigan Press, 1999.

Forge, Andrew, and Robert Gordon. *Claire Joyes and Jean-Marie Toulgouat, Monet at Giverny.* London, England: Mathews Miller Dunbar, 1975.

House, John. *Monet: Nature into Art*. New Haven, CT: Yale University Press, 1986.

Monet, Claude. *Monet by Himself.* Macdonald & Co, 1989.

Tucker, Paul Hayes. *Claude Monet: Life and Art.* Yale University Press, 1995.

Tucker, Paul Hayes, George T.M. Shackelford, and MaryAnne Stevens. *Monet in the 20th Century*. New Haven, CT: Yale University Press, 1998.

Wildenstein, Daniel. *Monet or the Triumph of Impressionism*. New York, NY: Taschen, 2014.

Wildenstein, Daniel. *Monet's Years at Giverny: Beyond Impressionism.* New York, NY: Metropolitan Museum of Art, 1978.

Index